WHITHORN, IONA AND LINDISFARNE
A Celtic Saga

Andrew R M Patterson MA, BD

THE SAINT ANDREW PRESS
EDINBURGH

First published in 1991 by
THE SAINT ANDREW PRESS
121 George Street, Edinburgh EH2 4YN

Copyright © Andrew R M Patterson 1991

ISBN 0 7152 0647 8

British Library Cataloguing in Publication Data
Patterson, Andrew
A Celtic saga.
1. Scotland. Strathclyde Region. Iona. Church of Scotland
religious communities. Iona Community, history
I. Title
267.185241423

ISBN 0-7152-0647 8

This book has been set in 10/12 pt Times.

The Publisher acknowledges financial assistance from
The Drummond Trust
towards the publication of this volume

Printed and Bound by Bell and Bain Ltd., Glasgow

CONTENTS

INTRODUCTION

WHITHORN, Iona and Lindisfarne are three very beautiful and remote places that have thankfully escaped the worst squalor of this industrial age of machines. Economic and environmental atrocities have barely touched them—they are and hopefully will remain good places to visit.

Each place is linked to the other by a shared history. From each the Celtic Church was nurtured in the dark centuries after the collapse of the Roman Empire. In those far-off days, before the onslaught of the Vikings and Normans—which created Scotland, Ireland, Wales and England—there were four peoples in these Islands: Cymri, Pict, Gael and Anglo-Saxon. They rivalled each other for control over the harvests which provided sustenance for the body; and for many years sporadic campaigns and skirmishes determined the border positions that defined the territories of each distinct community.

The mists of time have made the precise view of the events which established the Christian Gospel among these

warrior nations very hazy indeed. Written records from the period dating between the second and seventh centuries AD are sparse; thus very few details are known relating to the peoples who populated these Western Isles of Europe at that time. In the sixth century, however, there lived a monk in Wales called Gildas who chronicled the history of the Celtic peoples. Gildas came originally from Dumbarton in Scotland. And in the eighth century the Venerable Bede of Northumbria wrote his very detailed and carefully researched history of the English. Family trees and lists of kings of the various peoples also survive, as well as an exotic collection of stories about the lives of individual Saints—but all of these only provide a skeletal outline to the growth of the Celtic Church.

As a precise science, archaeology can flesh out the bare bones of our under-

1

standing. Careful sifting of the evidence can reveal much about how different groups of people made utensils, built shelters, farmed and fought. It is however much harder to untangle the riddle of how people actually *thought* and *believed*. Evidence gleaned from Christian burials may go a long way towards outlining the geographical spread of belief as found in the Gospel, but it does little more.

This booklet is therefore an attempt to explore the complex webs of faith that bind Whithorn, Iona and Lindisfarne in a shared and exciting history.

The first phase in the development of the Christian Church in these islands arose within the Roman province of *Britannia* (Britain), the land south of Hadrian's Wall. This earliest network of congregations did not survive for long the collapse of the commercial, administrative and military structures of the western Empire of the Romans in the early fifth century. Poor trade and sky-high inflation had already weakened the Empire. Entire tribes of Goths, Vandals, Franks and Huns, seizing the advantage, turned Europe into a battle-ground. In its wake, famine and plague stalked the survivors. Anglo-Saxon invaders followed suit and took the Roman province of *Britannia*, destroying the towns and ran-sacking villas which had erstwhile housed the Word and Sacrament of the first Christian sanctuaries.

The second phase in the development of the Church became the bid for its survival. This took place in the areas now known as Cornwall, Cumbria, Galloway and Strathclyde. These pockets of resistance remained free from Anglo-Saxon conquest. Even the Romans had not managed to yoke the tribes of these areas to their rule. Indeed fugitives from the destroyed towns of the defeated Roman province served to strengthen the membership of the Church among the Cymric tribes who successfully resisted the Anglo-Saxons.

Ninian of Whithorn in Galloway is best remembered among those early churchmen of the Cymri. In AD 398, 12 years before Rome withdrew its last legions from Britain, Ninian established the *See* (episcopal centre of church administration) of Galloway in Whithorn. The Gaels of Ireland were next to heed this Gospel entrusted to Whithorn.

As a result, Christian development moved into its third phase. This was due in large part to the work of a Cymric bishop in Ireland—a man called Patrick. Cymri, Pict and Gael alike looked to the work of Patrick for inspiration.

When Columba of Donegal landed on the Hebridean Island of Iona in AD 563, a fourth phase was entered into. The community he established there gained influence, rivalling even Ninian's Whithorn. And from Iona, the Gospel was taken to the Angles and Saxons of Northumbrian England.

Ninian, Patrick and Columba were just three of many whose work preserved the unbroken survival, and nurtured the new growth, of the Celtic Church at a time when the chaos of warfare throughout Europe threatened its very destruction. Whithorn, Iona and Northumbrian-based Lindisfarne were at the very heart of this defiance, proclaiming in the midst of extreme violence, with courage and quiet heroism, the faith, the hope and the love of Christ their King.

The following chapters take a concise look at the history of this achievement. All but cut off from contact with the central Church of Rome, the peoples of these far-off Islands developed a unique and wonderful exultancy in the divine, overcoming violence with the virtues of goodness and mercy. The legacy they bequeathed to us is one to remember now and for evermore.

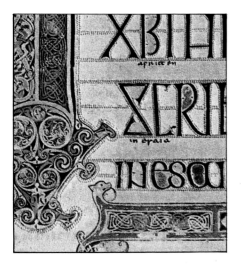

THE BARBARIAN
INVASIONS OF THE
ROMAN EMPIRE (5th cent AD)

PICTS

ANGLO-SAXONS

FRANKS

GOTHS

HUNS

WESTERN EMPIRE

ROME

EASTERN EMPIRE

BYZANTIUM

Trelipond

Jerusalem

ROMAN BRITANNIA
AND THE FIRST CHRISTIAN CONGREGATIONS
The First Four Centuries AD

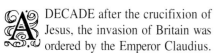 DECADE after the crucifixion of Jesus, the invasion of Britain was ordered by the Emperor Claudius. The huge resources of the Roman Empire, stretching from the Euphrates to the Rhine, were devoted to this enterprise. The military force of the Empire on land and at sea was well organised and highly advanced. Its destructive power was fearful. However, it met with unexpected and fierce resistance from the populous tribes of the Cymric Celts who inhabited southern Britain. War leaders, like Caractacus and Boadicea (*Boudicca*), led leagues of tribes against the legions of Rome.

The costs incurred by this resistance became too great, even for the mighty coffers of Rome. The north of the island was never conquered, nor was any attempt made to invade Ireland, although extended military occupation of the south of Britain made Boadicea's rebellion the last action from the southern Cymri.

These difficult enemies of Rome were a branch of the Celtic peoples. They were a warlike people who had emerged out of the great Eurasian grasslands of the East at the beginning of the last millennium BC, at the same time as Solomon was creating the famous Temple in Jerusalem. It is probable that adverse changes in climate had dried up Eurasia, driving its people out in search of new pastures for their life-giving flocks and herds. Some scholars, however, limit the origins of the Celts to what is known about the Halstatt and La Teine cultures which flourished along the upper Danube and Rhine from the eighth century BC.

In the course of their travels these ancestors of the Celts had acquired iron-working skills. The Celtic tribes appeared invincible as their power grew unmatched

Roman Foot Soldier

4

beside the Danube and the Rhine, before piercing through to the western seaboard of the continent.

The native born peoples of the Atlantic coastlands and the Western Isles of Europe were descended from those who had raised the henge stones and the *tumuli* (burial mounds) which dotted the landscape. Carnac, Stonehenge and Callanish are three well-known examples of the monuments built by those people who fought against the new Celtic men of iron. They had no knowledge of iron-working and their own bronze weapons could not resist the invaders.

Archaeological evidence, based on the analysis of pollen deposits, suggests that western Europe—like Eurasia—had suffered from a deteriorating climate. Intense volcanic activity in Iceland caused an atmospheric dust cloud to spread appallingly wet and cold conditions. Wide areas of upland countryside became blanketed with peat. The result was famine. There is also increasing evidence to suggest that at the same time as King David was reputed to have danced before the Tabernacle in the streets of Jerusalem, the north of Britain was becoming increasingly depopulated. Agriculture had become impossible.

Thus it was an ecological disaster which drove the Celts out of the continental heartland and fatally weakened the Bronze Age culture of western Europe.

Some of the invaders settled in what is now France, while others crossed the Pyrenees into the Iberian peninsula. Both of these colonising groups of Celts were to send settlers to the islands. From Iberia the Gaelic Celts came into Ireland, and from there to Scotland. And across the Channel came the Cymric Celts, who rose to dominance in Britain south of the Firth of Forth. They also established a significant presence in Ireland in rivalry with the Gaels.

North of the Forth, those distinctive people, the Picts, worked hard to protect

Ancient Henge Stones against the dawn sky

5

their independence. The Picts are still one of the mysteries of history. We do not know much about their origins or their language. Perhaps they were akin to the Basques of the Pyrenees, survivors of Bronze Age Europe in remote localities. Like the Basques, the Picts remained unconquered by Celtic or Roman invasion.

The Arabs have a saying: *My enemy's enemy is my friend.* When the legions of Rome attacked both Pict and Cymri in the north of Britain, a bond was created between the two peoples. Rome was now their common enemy, and not each other. In addition, the Picts had long since acquired the iron-working techniques of the Cymri, and various treaties and dynastic intermarriage had spread the Cymric language into the far north. A bond now seemed inevitable.

One hundred years after the birth of Christ, the Romans had subdued the Cymri over most of southern Britain, but attempts to conquer the Picts in their Grampian stronghold were not successful. One hundred years after the crucifixion of Christ, the Emperor Hadrian ordered the building of a defensive wall, which stretched from the Tyne to the Solway Firth, in order to secure the subjugated lands of the southern Cymri. Another frontier line was built from the Firth of Forth to the River Clyde in the time of the Emperor Antonine. Between Antonine's wall, made of turf, and the stone Hadrian's wall, the Romans tried to establish a buffer space between Roman *Britannia* and the Picts. This was the area of land which they called *Valentia*. The Romans encouraged some of the semi-independent Cymric principalities of that area to maintain their military structures against the Picts, while an astute mixture of bribe and threat encouraged the Cymri of Valentia to have many dealings with the Empire.

Behind the threat of the Roman legions came the wealth and show of the merchants, the land speculators and that breed of humanity which has always profiteered from the misery of conquered people. South of *Valentia* the forests were cleared in much the same way as they are today in the tropical rainforests. The dictat of a cash economy rose to prominence as expansive farming estates were established over wide areas of southern Britain.

The Celts had been largely pastoral people growing relatively little grain. It was not to be so in Roman *Britannia*. The Romans established huge estates which exported large crops of grain to the hungry millions in the cities of the Mediterranean. These estates were organised in ways that were very similar to the cotton and sugar plantations of the imperial slavery of the nineteenth century. *Britannia* became for the Romans a source of cheap raw materials: wheat, barley, wool, flax, timber, charcoal, copper, tin, leather, furs, hunting dogs, rare dyestuffs, river pearls, slaves and even gold.

The wharves of new boom towns, like London, were crammed with shipping. Sailors, speaking in foreign tongues reflecting the vastness of the Roman Empire, filled their holds with the riches of Britain.

The Greek poet Kazantzakis commented on the power and wealth of the Empire: *Rome sits upon the nations with her all-powerful, insatiable arms spread wide and receives the boats, caravans, goods and produce of all the world and all the sea. While believing in no God, she fearlessly and with ironic condescension receives the gods into her courts: from far away fire-worshipping Persia, Mithras, the sun-faced son of Ahuramasda mounted on the sacred bull which is soon to die; from the many uddered land of the Nile, Isis, who in springtime upon the blossoming fields seeks the fourteen pieces of her husband-brother Osiris, whom Typhon dismembered; from Syria, amidst heart-rending lament-ations, exquisite Adonis; from Phyrigia stretched out on a bier and covered with faded violets, Attis; from shameless Phoen-icia, Astarte of the thousand husbands; all the gods and phantoms of Asia and Africa, and from Greece white topped Olympus and black Hades ... 'what splendour, what irremovable joy to be omnipotent and im-mortal,' thinks Rome. Contented she smiles ... and forgets.*

For whom had Rome opened up the routes of land and sea? For whom had she toiled for so many ages to bring safety and peace to the world? From the wisdom of hindsight and believing in the providential power of the God of Israel as the One creator and moulder of history, the twentieth century observer has to answer—*for Christ!*

However, it was not all one-way trade on the wharves of London, or in the forum marketplaces of the fifty towns in Roman *Britannia*. The *Pax Romana* agreement ensured that wine, pottery, fine cloth and military supplies flowed into Britain.

The merchants were a cosmopolitan and far-travelled contribution to the Roman economy. Far-travelled also were the legions and auxiliaries that marched along the new roads of the province of *Britannia*. From Alexandria, Damascus, Carthage, Ephesus, Marseilles and Cologne, the soldiers poured in to serve in the most northerly frontier of the Roman Empire. In the marketplace and paradeground, ideas and conversation spread as rapidly as the international com-modities of commerce and war.

And so it was not long before the lit-erature and philosophy of the Hebrews filtered into Britain, accompanied by the new Gospel—the Gospel of Jesus, the Son of Man. Ironic though it may seem, it was the might of Rome which paved the way for the spread of the Gospel, keeping the sea-lanes and roads of the Empire safe from pirates and brigands, providing easier access along straighter routes, taking with it the way of the Lord.

Rome tolerated the religions of many peoples, as Kazantzakis described, but Christianity was certainly viewed with sus-picion as a dangerous and subversive creed. It was outlawed. Those who took bap-tismal vows of Church membership faced savage persecution. Early Christian congre-gations certainly did not advertise their existence to the secular authorities. Like Russian dissidents faced by Stalin's secret police—they did not dare to.

During the time of the Roman Empire, Christian men and women could not in all conscience proclaim loyalty to the State-sponsored religion which promoted the Emperor as a divine being. Periodically the streets of the towns and cities of every province in the Empire rang with the shriek-ing of *pogrom*—organised massacre—against these despised Christian subver-sives. It is not therefore surprising that there is little evidence of the earliest (and *illegal*) Church in Britain, but nothing seemed to stop the spread of this new creed and the hope it gave to people in such a brutal world.

Despite this persecution, it was the joy of the early Christians in the delight of their souls that shone out to attract far more converts than the cleverest words of their preachers in their huddled and secretive gatherings. The Gospel was listened to by the poor because of its call to justice, but it was the high-born and the free who also risked death by worshipping Christ in the company of slaves. In *Britannia*, as elsewhere, the courage of martyrs like Alban thwarted the intended effect of persecution.

In these first congregations, shared commonwealth was paramount over the private self in search of those things which moth and rust corrupt. With bread and wine they exulted in celebrations of peaceful love.

However, the Christians were not the only persecuted religious group in Britain. Before the Romans came, the Druids were the masters of the mysteries and the priestly sect of the Celtic tribes. Their role as

Roman Trade Ships

tribal intermediaries had made determined action by confederations of tribes against the Romans possible. Rome hated them because of this and made every effort to root out druidry from the south. But in *Valentia* and the moors of the west, the Druids survived—as they did in the far north and in Ireland. When so many other cults were being tolerated by the Romans, the Christians and Druids found common ground in the distinction they shared as the two religions which continued to be the target of sustained and brutal persecution.

Writing in the early third century AD, Origen of Alexandria, and Tertullian of Carthage, commented on the spread of Christianity in the island of Britain. Tertullian even stated that 'Christians can travel to areas that are inaccessible to Romans'. It seems probable that the influence of the Gospel had already spread beyond the borders of the most northerly province in the Empire and into the unconquered lands of the free Cymri.

The last great wave of *pogrom* and persecution against the Church took place at the end of the third century, during the reign of the Emperor Diocletian. It was said that bishops from Dumbarton and from Carlisle were murdered during this last massacre. All was changed in AD 313, when the Emperor Constantine issued his Edict of Milan. This was a declaration of a new toleration for the Church. Thus while the Roman State continued to tolerate the many religions of its people, the Christian Church had moved from the sufferance of official persecution to the enjoyment of a most-favoured status within the Empire. In actual fact, the Roman law was only just catching up with events, because the Church had become too widespread and influential to be vulnerable any longer to persecution.

In *Britannia*, south of Hadrian's wall, pagan basilicas became Christian churches. In this fourth century Church, the celibate ideals of monasticism were not as yet considered supreme. Many clerics were married men living with their families.

This Church was woven into the complex strands of the Empire, but the power of Rome was already beginning to unravel. Commerce and trade had gone into decline. In addition, the climate of the planet had begun to get worse again, as it had in those distant days of David and Solomon, when the Celts had been forced by famine to move out of Eurasia. People began to flood westwards out of the east. The struggle to stem this human tide coming up the Danube caused the Empire to reduce its garrison in *Britannia*. In AD 367, the Picts marched through *Valentia* and invaded the weakened south, even pillaging London. The Picts were driven back by the Romans, but on the continent disaster followed disaster. Roman Europe had become a battleground.

Anglo-Saxon mercenaries from Germany had been brought to *Britannia* by the Romans in the attempt to drive the Picts back. When these troops mutinied in the early fifth century and sent for their kin from the north German coastlands, Roman *Britannia* itself became a battleground. These Anglo-Saxon mutineers and their descendants made Roman *Britannia* into their England. Once the violence of immediate warfare had ended, the poor peasantry and estate slaves of the Romans were only exchanging the greed of one set of masters for that of the new; but for the province of *Britannia*, international trade and the cash crop economy were now at an end. The invaders had no use for the Roman towns which had thrived on commerce. These were destroyed, and the Church of the basilicas and villas was obliterated, apart from the lands which the Cymri still kept free in the north and west: in the northern *Valentia,* where Galloway, Lothian and Strathclyde had their kingdoms; and in the west in what is now Cumbria, Wales and Cornwall.

Cut off by war from the Roman south of Europe, the Cymri of Britain were set to continue into the future *with* their Church; both the Church and the Cymri were to prove the most most durable survivors of the Roman Age.

THE SURVIVAL OF THE CHURCH
IN THE LANDS OF THE CYMRI
The Fifth Century AD

LEGENDS echo down the centuries about a Cymric war leader called Arthur who drove back the Anglo-Saxons. These legends also speak to us of the Cymric tribes of Cornwall, Wales, Cumbria, Strathclyde and Galloway, who defended their language, culture and society with considerable success for hundreds of years.

These areas had never been fully integrated into the Roman Empire. Indeed, their own military structures *outlasted* the Roman military machine as it slowed down, faltered and finally collapsed. The free tribesmen of the northern and western moors knew the trade of war better than the townsmen and agricultural slaves of Roman *Britannia*. And the Anglo-Saxon conquerors of the south and east found the Cymric tribes formidable enemies.

In AD 398, just twelve years before the withdrawal of the last regular troops of the Empire from Britain, a priest was on his way home to Galloway from Rome. He had studied in Rome for ten years, and had been consecrated a bishop there. This priest, called Ninian, was travelling through a Europe whose economy and social structure were already beginning to break down, even *before* the warfare and barbarian invasion which was set to complete the final destruction.

On his way home to his people in Galloway, Ninian rested at the monastic community founded by Martin of Tours. Communities on the continent, like that of Martin and the later Benedict, were to be the bastions of Christianity which ensured the survival of the Church throughout the disastrous wars of the fifth century. Martin and the monastic ideal greatly influenced Ninian.

A Roman Cavalry officer

10

The dominant tribe of Galloway at that time was the Novantae. They controlled the lands west of the Annan up to the Carrick hills. They used great ox-drawn ploughs for cultivating grain, but were primarily a pastoral people with a passion for livestock in general and horses in particular. As allies of the Romans against the Picts, they had learned and used the latest innovations in the military technology of the Empire—including the use of the stirrup.

The Romans had discovered the stirrup during their long warfare against the Persian Empire. Roman generals were swift to adopt this innovation which had made the Persian cavalry so effective. Before this, the use of cavalry had been limited to mounted archers or swiftly deployed troops who then fought on foot, or who were used to harry a fleeing enemy. With the stirrup to steady him in the saddle, a mounted man could withstand the shocking impact of a horse crashing into infantry. New military tactics were evolved. Even the tight discipline of the foot soldiers of the legions lost their supremacy because of the stirrup.

Thus the fourth century saw the development of heavy cavalry units mounted on the largest available horses.

We do not know if the Cymric tribes of Britain inherited any of this bloodline of heavy horses from the Romans, but we do know that the Cymri used fast-moving and heavy-hitting cavalry to withhold the advances of the Anglo-Saxons. (See, for example, 'The Ride of the Goddodin', an ancient Welsh poem.)

The Galloway in which Ninian lived faced enemies other than the forefathers of the English who came marauding over the Pennines. Anxious to claim their share of the spoils, the Gaels of Ireland came too. The Galloway coast commanded the seas across which the Gaels plundered; and in Ninian's day the long peninsula of the Machars stretched south into the tideway. There, the Novantae built a chain of headland forts to provide a first line of defence and to raise the alarm when raiders approached. The Gaels, however, although able to establish a colony in Argyle, could not establish a presence in Galloway. Their attempt to colonise the Lleyn Peninsula in

Wales was also defeated by the Cymri.

Thus it appears that Ninian lived in a land and among a people who were well prepared for war. Behind their defence the Church he served put down roots and began to flourish.

He began by organising the building of a church at Whithorn in the Machars, which was called *Candida Casa*. The literal translation from the Latin does not mean 'a white house'; if so, its Latin name would have been *Alba Casa*. *Candida* means 'shining, luminous, glistening white'. It was the word which Jerome used in the Vulgate Bible to translate the appearance of the robe of Jesus at the transfiguration. *Candida Casa* refers perhaps less to the architectural qualities of the building and more to the spiritual atmosphere that was experienced in the place which the Northumbrians were to call *Hwit herne* in their language, or 'White House of Ninian', which became the *Whithorn* of history.

At Whithorn, in the strongly defended lands of the Novantae, Ninian's work in Word and Sacrament flourished in a safe haven. From this land, luminous with spiritual power and influence, the literary scholarship, healing arts, craftsmanship, international outreach, beauty and hope that are the hallmarks of the Gospel began to flourish among the Cymri.

The Druids had taught in their earlier understanding that the souls of the dead travelled away westward beyond the sunset to the land of *Tir-nan-Og*, the land of eternal youth. Their deity of the sea, *Manannan Macher* (or *MacLir*), guided the soul on its journey from this world to the next, in the same way as the boatman Charon in Olympian mythology, who ferried the souls of the dead to Hades.

The pre-Christian cult of *Mannanan* is still evoked by geographical landmarks of the Solway. The burgh of Annan, and the Isle of Man, are memorials in the derivation of their names. Many think that the origin for the name of the long peninsula of the Machars is from the Gaelic *Machair* which means pasture-land. Others think that the Machars derived its name from *Manannan Macher*. If this is true, it seems that Ninian was establishing his episcopal See in the heartland of the druidic cult.

Whatever the derivation of the modern place-name, there appears to have been little bitterness and less violence in the dealings of the first Celtic Church with supporters of the native religion, who perhaps saw the Isle of Man and the long peninsula of the Machars as the gateways to the *Tir-nan-Og* of the sacred voyage.

Centuries of persecution by pagan authorities had left the main Church of the Mediterranean deeply suspicious of all non-Hebrew religious insights. The Greek Pan of the horns and cloven hooves, the divinity who symbolised natural forces, was translated into the fire and brimstone of Lucifer's myth because of this suspicion. However, among the Celts of the Solway there was no such atmosphere of suspicion. In peaceful and mutual interchange of ideas, Ninian conversed with the Druid brotherhood among the tribes, and many of the Druids came to Christianity, bringing with them into the Church a whiff of druidry.

Ninian and his friends did not only work in Galloway. They travelled throughout what is now southern Scotland (Roman *Valentia)*, and into the Strathmore of the

Picts, beyond the Tay. Not once did druidry offer them violence or refuse them a welcome. However, although many people remained loyal to the old ways, and druidry survived as a major force among the Cymri and Picts until the seventh century, Ninian's Church formed a sure foundation upon which the later Church would be built.

However, this Cymric Church made few attempts to work among the worst enemies of their people, the Anglo-Saxons, who had brought the sword and fire to Roman *Britannia*. The Venerable Bede, in his History of the English, rebukes this earliest Church in the north for this failure: the chasm of enmity between the two peoples had become too great to cross.

Meanwhile, although the Druids may have tolerated and even admired the early Christian congregations, the Anglo-Saxons offered them nothing but violence.

The next stage in the development of the Church in these islands was not among the conquering Anglo-Saxons of England. The Gospel was to travel first from the Cymri to the Gaels of Ireland.

THE GOSPEL IN IRELAND
The Fifth Century AD

ST PATRICK is forever linked with the island of Ireland, but he was in actual fact a man of Britain. The son of a priest, he was raised to believe in the Christian God. Patrick was born before Ninian returned to Whithorn from Rome, at a time when the Empire was still militarily powerful. Many priests at this time were married men living with

their families. The monastic ideal of celibacy was not yet widespread.

Both the Clyde and the Solway have claims to the birthplace of Patrick. Some say that his childhood was lived near the old replenishing base of the Roman navy at Dumbarton. Dumbarton, at the north west of *Valentia*, had become the greatest military base of the Strathclyde Cymri. Others claim that Patrick came from the upper Solway near the Roman town of Carlisle, at the western end of Hadrian's wall.

However, all the traditions associated with Patrick agree that he was captured by slave-raiding Gaelic pirates from Ireland. Any piracy so close to the Roman military bastion of Dumbarton would have been a bit like stirring a hornets' nest with a stick. On the other hand, the wide estuarine expanse of the upper Solway made good pirate waters, full of creeks and reedy chan-

nels that were the haunts of smugglers and bandits from Roman to recent times. However, whether born near the Clyde or the Solway, Patrick was certainly a child of *Valentia* and from the same people as Ninian.

During the period when Ninian was bishop of Galloway, Patrick was a slave. But he eventually escaped and returned to Britain after a harsh adolescence spent in miserable years of exile. Once more among his own people, Patrick trained for the priesthood. His training was not the same as Ninian had in the city of Rome. *Valentia* was cut off from the Mediterranean by a Europe at war with itself, and thus it was a rustic type of Latin that Patrick learned, even though some authorities maintain that he studied for a time in the war-torn Roman province of northern Gaul.

The Church had been much influenced

by the monastic ideals which Ninian had brought from the monastery at Tours, founded by Martin. Perhaps also the ideal of monastic celibacy, which Patrick was to embrace, had other more native-born roots.

Druids spent long years of training as they memorised the unwritten teachings of their earlier folklore. They lived an almost collegiate life with their fellows, but they also travelled far among the clans and tribes of Celtic society. The Druids were not settled family-type men, and neither was Patrick.

Some strange compulsion caused this young priest to return to Ireland. His arrival and settlement on the east coast of Ulster was like the falling of the first pebble that leads to a great avalanche of change. The people of Ireland listened to the Gospel. Many were enlightened by it.

There is a story told about Patrick stand-ing before the High King of Ireland being closely questioned by an audience of Druids. They wanted him to give them an explanation which they could accept, of the Christian doctrine of the Trinity. The gathering in the presence of the High King was largely of Gaelic Celts. They were the dominant people in that island, although there were still enclaves of Picts and Cymri as there were in Britain. Patrick spoke Gael-ic fluently from his years of slavery. Before he spoke to the people about the Trinity, he stooped and plucked a three-leafed clover, a shamrock. With this he instructed the most powerful in the land about the One in Three and the Three in One. High King, nobility and druidry listened to Patrick's teachings and many were convinced.

Throughout his long life Patrick travel-led the length and breadth of Ireland, but his base was in the Ards peninsula beside those mountains of Mourne which are visible from the Machars. His neighbours were the Picts and Cymri of eastern Ulster, but the message he had brought gained a new vibrancy and energy among the Gaels.

Whilst the Gospel was transforming the life of Ireland throughout the fifth century AD, the Cymri of Britain struggled to hold back the Anglo-Saxons. Gildas, the monk from Dumbarton, recorded these times of conflict. Arthur, the fact behind the legend, was one of their war leaders at the end of this century. He drove the Anglo-Saxons back over the Pennines and even cam-paigned in the Thames Valley, the very heartland of the new English power.

The Church in Ireland thus thrived in this time of peace; and from its shores the Good News returned to mainland Britain with renewed strength and vigour.

IONA AND THE GAELIC CHURCH IN BRITAIN
The Sixth Century AD

N AD 561, a sea-going coracle—*curragh*—was launched into the River Foyle, beside the oak groves where the modern city of Londonderry has been built. Chief among the small company of men who were to crew the vessel was a prince of the O'Neil clan of Donegal. He was to be known to later centuries as Columba. His voyage through the Hebrides to Iona has had at times as large a grip upon the human imagination as the Argosy of Jason.

But Columba was seeking more than a golden fleece from the teeth of a dragon, however: he was seeking the place of his resurrection, for he was a man burdened with guilt and remorse.

By then in his forties, Columba had been a priest of the Gaelic Church for nearly two decades. In his youth he had studied under a great scholar called Fin-nian. Finnian had taught for many years at Whithorn, and he had a rare and precious collection of manuscripts he had legitimately copied in the library of the '*magnum monasterium*' of the Machars. Finnian had settled in the Ards peninsula of eastern Ulster and the youthful Columba had studied with him among the Picts and Cymri of the east coast.

Columba later left Finnian to work in Donegal among his own people, but he coveted Finnian's manuscript of the Book of Psalms and attempted to make a copy of this manuscript without having first gained Finnian's permission. He was caught. Finnian was outraged at the behaviour of his former pupil and he appealed to Diarmid, the High King of Ireland. Diarmid made a judgment in this dispute between the two clerics. It is in fact one of the earliest precedents of copyright law known to history:

'*To each cow belongs her calf. To each book belongs her copy*'. Diarmid ordered Columba to give Finnian the illicit copy of the Psalms. Columba refused to accept this judgment. The result was open warfare. At *Culdreimhne* in AD 560 the two opposing factions met in battle. Hundreds were killed and maimed. Irish Picts and Cymri who had supported Finnian suffered more than the Gaels out of Donegal who had supported Columba in his quarrel.

Clan warfare was not new to Ireland and the rivalry between Cymri, Pict and Gael was an old story even before the killing at *Culdreimhne*. But the work of Patrick in Ireland was more than a century old by AD 560; the preaching of the beatitudes of Jesus had changed and gentled Celtic society from its earlier cruelty and violence. No wonder Christian sentiment in Ireland was appalled and horrified at all this killing over a quarrel between two priests. Lay and clerical opinion alike rebuked Columba harshly.

Columba sailed out of the Foyle determined to win as many people for Christ as had been lost at the battle. So this northern Argosy began, whose Trezipond was to be the small island of Iona.

The earlier wave of Gaelic piracy which had resulted in the capture of Patrick had been thwarted by the strong defences of Galloway. A Gaelic attempt to colonise northern Wales was also driven back with great loss, but colonists out of Gaelic Ireland were more successful in the sparsely-populated fjords, islands and peninsulas of Argyle. There, throughout the fifth and sixth centuries, pirates nests became settled communities. The western Picts, whose stronghold was beside Loch Etive under Ben Cruachan, were unable to drive back the land-hungry Gaelic families who sailed over from Donegal and Antrim.

These people in the first precarious Gaelic colony in Britain were Columba's kin. During the time of the *Culdreimhne* quarrel, his cousins in Argyle had been similarly preoccupied with matters of war. In AD 560, King Brude of the northern Picts led a great army into Argyle. Gabran, King of the Gaels, was killed and his army scattered. Thus when Columba sailed to Argyle, he had to travel first to King Brude in Inverness to seek permission to settle in Iona. This was granted: in AD 563, after two years of uncertain wandering, Columba and his companions settled in Iona.

Columba, of the royal clan of Donegal, had status because of his birth, but he also had other qualities which aroused love and respect in those who knew him. When Columba began his work from Iona, the Gaels of Argyle were a defeated people.

Peaceful times on Iona

And so, in addition to his spiritual responsibilities, he guided the political life of this Gaelic colony. In their weakened state they had much to fear from the Picts of King Brude and also from the Cymric people of Strathclyde who bordered Argyle to the south and east. Perhaps Columba felt remorse that when King Brude had attacked them, no help had come from Ireland—they were all too preoccupied with the *Culdreimhne* war.

And thus, ironically, although Columba had been the instigator of war in Ireland, in northern Britain he was to become the peacemaker between Gael, Pict and Cymri.

For the first eleven years of Columba's exile from Ireland, Argyle was ruled by Conaill. In AD 574 Aehdan became the King of that land. At his investiture he was consecrated by Columba who officiated at the service as leader of the spiritual community of Iona at that time. During the reign of King Conaill, Argyle had been recovering from defeat. But under Aehdan it was different. He was a warrior who meddled in the affairs not only of the Picts and the Cymri, but who also kept a close watch on the manoeuvres of the Northumbrian English. Aehdan tried to set each against the other, always trying to increase the relative power of Argyle.

King Roderick of Strathclyde was the leader of the northern Cymri at that time. Annoyed at Aehdan's scheming, he threatened an invasion of Argyle. Columba, having gone to Inverness to act as ambassador for Argyle to King Brude, now had to travel to Strathclyde to deploy his considerable diplomatic skills to placate the northern Cymri.

Roderick was a Christian who ruled Strathclyde, Galloway, Cumbria and Lothian. Because of his alliance with Maelgan of Wales, the High King of all the Cymri in Britain, Roderick and his allies were a real threat to the Gaels in Argyle. Roderick had already inflicted sharp defeats upon the Northumbrians, killing their King Ida. It seemed that Columba had much to fear from the Cymri. Were the Gaels to be driven from Argyle as they had been by Maelgan's ancestors in Wales?

Columba arranged a meeting with Roderick's great friend Kentigern, nick-named Mungo, the bishop of Glasgow. At this meeting Columba and Mungo exchanged croziers, the staves which were the symbols of their pastoral authority. This significant act established mutual recognition and inter-communion between the Churches of two peoples who had often been locked in battle. At last Columba, the warmonger of Ireland, had atoned for *Culdreimhne* in this most significant of peacemaking gestures.

Columba was not always as friendly with the Cymric Church however. Shortly before he died in AD 597, another company of clerics arrived in Iona. Their leader was Donnan, a graduate of Whithorn. They wished to establish a community in the northern Hebrides. Other Cymric missions had already gone to Orkney and Shetland. Donnan came to Iona seeking Columba's blessing on their venture. He asked Columba to be his *anamchara*, his soul-friend and spiritual counsellor. But according to later traditions, Columba refused, saying, perhaps prophetically, that he would not be a soul-friend to a company of red-martyrdom. The red-martyrdom of public execution had been horribly well known in the early, illegal Church of the Roman Empire. Many Cymric priests, nuns, monks and other Christian people had been executed in their borderlands by the barbarous and pagan English. Away from the English, red-martyrdom among both the Cymric and the Gaelic branches of the Celtic Church, however, had been little known since the time of Ninian and Patrick.

Donnan and his company were undeterred by their cold welcome on Iona. They sailed north and established a community on the island of Eigg. In AD 619 Columba's prophecy that they would meet 'red-martyrdom' seemed to be fulfilled when a raiding party of unknown origin slaughtered Donnan's community. The Celtic world was horrified.

Perhaps too in refusing Donnan 'soul-friendship', Columba was denying the inter-communion and mutual recognition of the sacrament of the eucharist at each other's hands. Columba's earlier agreement with Kentigern seems to have applied only to Strathclyde. Columba was thus sending a message to the Church of Whithorn that the Hebrides and the northwest were out of bounds. The only spiritual authority which would be tolerated there would be that of the Gaelic Church, exerted from Iona.

By AD 619, after Donnan's murder in the Hebrides, the power of the Cymri was on the wane, even though it was to resurge later in the century. Roderick was long dead and his anti-English pact had ended in complete disarray. The seventh century was to see Northumbria and Wessex this time grow to a greater strength than Cornwall, Wales, Cumbria, Galloway and Strathclyde —far greater than they could resist. The English Kingdoms were to dominate over the Cymri, but they themselves were to be overrun by a power even the English shield-wall could not oppose—the power of God. The long defence of the Cymri by those like the half-remembered Arthur, Gawain, Percival and Lancelot had not been in vain.

When the weight of English wealth and numbers finally caused the Cymri to cry out for peace, the English themselves had bent the knee to Christ, and their Kings were baptised men who heeded the Gospel demand for mercy. The barbarity of total war and massacre was at an end, and peace treaties, written and witnessed by Christian clerics, were enacted between the Cymri and the English kingdoms.

Ninian's legacy of Word and Sacrament had been taken to the Gaels by Patrick. This legacy had grown in worth and stature in Ireland, spreading from Columba's Iona throughout the north and beyond. In large part, the heeding of the Gospel by the English was because of Iona and Columba's achievements. The debt of *Culdreimhne* had been repaid. Gael, Pict, Cymri and Anglo-Saxon began to share a common culture. The Church began to guide their Kings who became more than marauding war-leaders. Consecrated and anointed by the Church at their coronations, they were now Christian monarchs who shared a common culture of worship and ethical standard. The inter-nationalism of the Church had bridged the national rivalries within these western isles of Europe.

Blessed indeed were the peacemakers of those times, the men and women who were part of that great outpouring of love which conquered the hatred of war.

THE TAMING OF THE ENGLISH BY THE GOSPEL
The Seventh and Eighth Centuries AD

THE VENERABLE Bede of Northumbria wrote his History of the English Church in the early decades of the eighth century. In the History he reviewed the achievements of the Gospel among his people in the previous century. In his day, the peoples of England were subject to several small kingdoms. In the south, Wessex was of most importance after its long wars with the Cornish and the Welsh. The great forests of the midlands were contained within the realm of Mercia, and the kingdoms of Kent and Anglia controlled the lands on either side of the Thames estuary. From the Humber to the Tees stretched the great kingdom of Northumbria. It had broken the Cymric defence along the Pennines, and ruled along the west coast from the Mersey to Morecambe Bay.

Roman *Britannia* was a thing of the past. In its place a new nation was developing, even though the English kingdoms made war on each other as well as against the Cymri. But Bede tells how, from Kent to Northumbria, the Gospel transformed the English, taming their violence towards each other and towards their neighbours in these islands.

At the beginning of the seventh century, the English had been fighting against the Christian Cymri of the west for two centuries, and they had not been receptive to the Gospel preached by their enemies who had so often brought fire and ruin to the pioneering English hamlets. The Gospel therefore had to find other routes into their national life.

In AD 597 a bishop from Rome called Augustine settled in Kent. On the continent, the Mediterranean Church had already survived the cataclysm of barbarian invasion, and strong kings in Merovingian

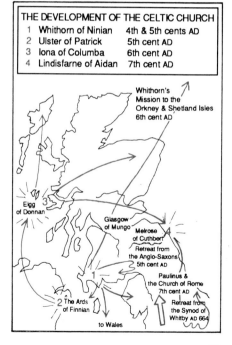

THE DEVELOPMENT OF THE CELTIC CHURCH
1	Whithorn of Ninian	4th & 5th cents AD
2	Ulster of Patrick	5th cent AD
3	Iona of Columba	6th cent AD
4	Lindisfarne of Aidan	7th cent AD

Whithorn's Mission to the Orkney & Shetland Isles 6th cent AD

Eigg of Donnan

Glasgow of Mungo

Melrose of Cuthbert

Retreat from the Anglo-Saxons 5th cent AD

Paulinus & the Church of Rome 7th cent AD

Retreat from the Synod of Whitby AD 664

2 The Ards of Finnian

to Wales

France were bringing a new peace in which the Church could develop. Previous to this, the Cymric and the Gaelic Churches had had very little contact with the Roman Church. They had survived in isolation away from the developing conventions of the continental Church. Through Augustine's ministry in Canterbury, the mainstream ecclesiastical forms of worship and administration were to rise to dominance in the England of Bede.

Augustine and his Roman missionaries were to base their work in the royal households of England, but the Gospel did not only spread throughout England as a result of the work of Canterbury. The Gospel also flooded in from the north, throughout Northumbria and into Mercia. The influence of the Gaelic Church of Iona was to be felt as far south as the Thames valley.

Bede records how Iona came to have a guiding hand on the affairs of the Northumbrians. King Aedhan, whom Columba consecrated, was called 'Aedhan the False' by the Cymri. This was because in his rivalry with the Picts and the kingdoms of Strathclyde, he was prepared to make a pact with the barbaric Northumbrians.

After the death of the powerful King Ethelfrid in AD 617, a dynastic rivalry caused a murderous dispute in the royal house of Northumbria. Two princes, only young boys, had to flee from their uncle who had seized the throne. Eventually the fugitives sought sanctuary on Iona. Like Patrick, these boys spent their adolescence in exile among a foreign people. On Iona they were raised as Christians. The dynastic tides of Northumbria changed and the oldest prince, Oswald, returned to his people and became their King—a Christian King.

Once established on his throne, in 632, Oswald sent to Iona for missionaries to help establish the Church in Northumbria.

The first deputation from Iona met with little success. Returning baffled, they pleaded that the Northumbrians were too crude and cruel a people ever to heed the Gospel. A second deputation was led by a priest called Aidan. Language was a barrier at first, with King Oswald having to translate the Gaelic of Aidan's preaching, phrase by phrase, until the Celtic churchmen became fluent in the language of Northumbria.

Slowly but surely the message of the Gospel was understood.

Northumbria was ruled from the great fortress of Bamburgh and from the royal township of Yetholm in the Cheviots, guardians of the disputed moors to the north and west from which the Cymri had attacked so often in their deadly raids. Close to Yetholm and Bamburgh was the tidal island of Lindisfarne. Celtic clerics often chose remote places surrounded by water for their monastic settlements. Thus it was that Aidan chose Lindisfarne to establish a monastic settlement that mirrored the life on Iona.

Lindisfarne, and not the Royal Court, was the base from which the Gaelic mission to the north of England was sustained. Whereas Augustine and the Roman Church at first preferred to live among the nobility, the Celtic missionaries out of Lindisfarne lived austere lives, poorer than the poor. English ploughmen and their families loved them for this and heeded their Gospel.

It is said that King Oswald gave to Aidan out of the Royal stables a splendid horse of fine pedigree. Aidan gave the horse to the first poor family he met, preferring to conduct his mission on two feet, as did his master, Jesus, the carpenter of Nazareth.

Oswald was a friend of saints, but he was also the leader of his people. In AD 642, he was killed in battle against a pagan army which came from Mercia. His brother, Oswy, had been with him during the years on Iona and it was Oswy who drove back the invaders. After that, Oswald's young brother ruled Northumbria for nearly thirty years. Throughout his reign Lindisfarne grew in stature and began to rival the achievements of Whithorn and Iona.

Even with the patronage of Kings, Aidan's work in Northumbria cannot have been easy. The historian, Arthur Bryant, has described the early English in the following terms:

Lindisfarne

They loved fighting. Their poetry, chanted in the mead halls of their chieftains as they sat feasting at long tables, is full of the clash of the 'hammered blades', 'the serried bucklers', 'the shields of linden wood', of 'arrows sleeting like hail.' They loved the symbols of death and carnage; the raven who followed the host, his beak dripping with blood, the hungry hawks hovering over the battlefield, the funeral pyre hung with shields and helmets round which the companions of the fallen sang the joys of war and the warrior virtues.'

These were the people who had once been the foes of the Christian Cymri, whose fathers at Chester, under King Ethelfrid in 613, had murdered over one thousand monks during the Northumbrian invasion of Wales. Even their word for *church* was derived from their word for *plunder*. These were the people who had listened to the powerful words of Aidan, translated phrase by phrase for their understanding by their King, Oswald.

Aidan spoke of Christ as a leader who had been brave and true, who had offered his followers a freeman's choice between good and evil, and a hero's reward for those who were faithful. This appealed to their warrior ethic of loyalty. But Aidan also preached on the other virtues of Jesus, those that were no more common among English warriors than they had been among the pre-Christian Celts: *Love* not Hate, *Gentleness* not Force, *Mercy* not Vengeance. These had been the weapons with which Christ the Hero had gained the victory. The Northumbrians own courage in battle was small indeed when compared with the steadfastness of Christ before the Cross.

Through the Gospel, Aidan and Oswald offered the Northumbrians a hope and purpose that had not been present in their earlier beliefs of stoic endurance before the Fates. Through the Celtic Church, Northumbrians learned that they did not inhabit a universe without compassion. The mighty God of Israel loved all nations and all people, and God had ransomed this world out of the clutches of evil through the life and work of Jesus. The Holy Spirit of the God who made the shamrock was with them in every breath and beat of the pulse.

At the same time that Oswald sent to Iona for missionaries to evangelise his kingdom, another group of churchmen was making its way from Canterbury into the Vale of York. Paulinus was their leader. Like Augustine he was a Roman from Italy. Like Aidan he was a man of peace who travelled unarmed through a warlike kingdom.

For two centuries after the military collapse of Rome, the Church in these western isles of Europe had developed in isolation. Aidan of Lindisfarne represented the island traditions; whereas Paulinus at York represented the continental mainstream that looked to Rome, and the bishop of Rome, as the ultimate arbiter of ecclesiastical authority.

In AD 603, six years after Augustine began his mission in Kent, the Bishop of Canterbury met with a deputation of seven bishops from the native Cymric Church of Wales. It was not a happy meeting. Augustine had been originally entrusted by Pope Gregory with the conversion of the English. He had arrived in Britain armed with the latest customs and practices of the Church of Rome. Augustine fully expected the Welsh bishops to accept his authority simply because he had been sent by the Pope. The Welsh, however, were not prepared to accept the authority of the Bishop of Canterbury over them and the meeting with Augustine ended in uproar.

There were other bones of contention. The Welsh bishops, in common with their kin in the north, and the Gaelic and Pictish Churches, calculated the date for Easter in the same way as the Orthodox Church of the East still does. However the Roman

Church had decided upon a new method for calculating the Pascal celebrations. Alone in Western Europe, the native Churches of the islands of Britain still held to the old practice. Celtic churchmen also wore a different style of tonsure from that of the Roman churchmen, and the style and flavour of their liturgical worship was out of step with the Church of Rome.

Tension arose between Canterbury and the Celts as a result of these differences. The same tensions were to be found between the York of Paulinus and Aidan's Lindisfarne. Oswald and Oswy remained loyal to the ways of Iona, because of their upbringing among the Gaels. However, Oswy had married a lady who had been baptised by the Roman Church. The obvious confusion caused by Easter being celebrated on two different occasions by two competing religious factions in the royal household was unsatisfactory for all concerned.

In 664 a great conference was convened at Whitby to resolve the problem. On a headland above the sea, a princess known as Hilda, of the royal Northumbrian line, had established a great religious community. She was its abbess. She subscribed to Roman practice. Hilda, like many other women in the early Church (for example, the great abbess Bridget of Kildare who continued the work of Patrick of Ireland) had a huge influence on the Whitby proceedings.

The Northumbrians loved the men of Lindisfarne, but Hilda and Wilfred, the Roman bishop of Ripon, presented their case with a sophistication that the Celtic churchmen could not hope to match. King Oswy ruled in favour of the Roman arguments, a fact which the Venerable Bede recorded with great satisfaction. He presented the Celtic faction in his History as well-intentioned, but wrong-headed and primitive.

Thus after Whitby, it was York and not Lindisfarne that was to be the centre of the northern English Church. Northumbrian power had enforced the decision of Whitby, in favour of Roman practice, upon Lindisfarne, and also upon the see of Whithorn in Galloway. Iona and the Pictish Church were to remain loyal to the old customs for a few more generations, however; but even in Ireland, Roman practices became dominant, with the Cornish and Welsh likewise coming into agreement, along with their Wessex neighbours.

In the same fateful year of 664, a terrible plague spread throughout the islands of Britain. This 'yellow plague' brought about an unhappy start to the new Church policy of conformity with Rome: tens of thousands died from the contagion which held no respect for man-made frontiers.

King Oswy died in 670 and was succeeded by Egfrid. The new King set his mind to extending the power of Northumbria against the Picts, Gaels and Cymri of the north. This policy of enforcing religious conformity with the spiritual authority of York resulted in as great a disaster for an English army as Bannockburn was all those centuries later. For in 686, at Nechtanesmere in Strathmore, a Northumbrian army was totally destroyed by the Picts, enraged by Egfrid's actions.

The two decades between the Synod of Whitby and the battle of Nechtanesmere were difficult for Lindisfarne. Many of the community, including the Abbot Colman, stubbornly remained loyal to the old Celtic practices and returned to Iona. Lindisfarne perhaps only survived this time of transition because of the life and work of its abbot and bishop who died the year after Nechtanesmere.

Bishop Cuthbert was raised in the Lammermuir hills on the borderland between English Northumbria and Cymric Strathclyde. He was trained at the Celtic monastery of Melrose where he nearly died of the 'yellow plague' in the wake of the Synod of Whitby. Cuthbert's leadership at Lindisfarne ensured that the exultant faith of Celtic spirituality was not completely squeezed out of the Northumbrian Church.

A very young Bede is supposed to have met the aged Cuthbert. Bede may have been biased in favour of Roman Church procedure, but he was always warm in his praises of Aidan and Cuthbert, Columba and Ninian, even though he censured the stubbornness of his Celtic contemporaries, deploring their single-mindedness.

The eighth century after Christ, in which Bede was writing, was a golden age for the four peoples of northern Britain. The Scots of Argyle (as the Gaelic colonists were called), the Picts north of the Forth, the Cymri of Cumbria, Galloway and Strathclyde, and the English of Northumbria, continued to strive for advantage over each other, but Nechtanesmere had set a limit to English ambitions. Bede records the peace that became the norm.

The Church of Christ gave common ground to all in their dealings with each other. Christian virtues moderated the violence of the warrior creeds and the arts of peace flourished under the stewardship of the Church. It was a Church of saints and sinners, ploughmen and kings, men and women in their generations. Those were years of beauty and gentleness.

DRAGONSHIPS AND THE VIKINGS
The Ninth Century AD

IN AD 800 the Emperor Charlemagne was consecrated by the Pope. From the hills of Saxony to the Pyrenees, Europe accepted his authority. The Saracens of Iberia who followed the way of Islam were held in the south, but out of the north a new fury was about to descend.

The seventh and eighth centuries had seen a golden age in the life of the Church of Britain, but they were also centuries of fine weather with bumper harvests throughout the whole continent. Populations had grown. But then, with little warning, the climatic conditions began to deteriorate, harvests became thin. Famine came to the marginal lands of northern Europe. Scandinavia in particular was very badly hit.

Driven by hunger as well as greed—first as pirates and then as colonists—the Vikings came. From Sicily to the Hebrides, the whole of Europe was to live in fear of incessant and brutal attacks from the north.

In AD 793 Lindisfarne had been attacked by pirates. In 802, Iona was also laid to waste. Celtic churchmen, often deliberately choosing islands for their settlements, were to find that such areas proved horribly vulnerable to this new threat as the Viking dragonships searched them out.

The Viking work *kerke* was similar to the Anglo-Saxon word *church*. In language and in custom, these later Vikings were very similar to the earlier Anglo-Saxons who had destroyed the Roman Church of *Britannia* four centuries earlier. *Kerke* and *church* meant *plunder*. It took time for the word to acquire new meaning in each respective language.

All four peoples in the island of Britain—Gaelic Scot, Pict, Cymri and Anglo-Saxon—were to suffer from this second great wave of Germanic invasion from the coastlines of northern Europe. This time it was not Roman basilicas that were devoured by flame and plunder. This time it was the smoke rising above the pyres of Lindisfarne, York, Iona and Whithorn which obscured the sky. The tide of 'red-martyrdom' again flowed around the shores of the western isles of Europe.

The story of the taming of the Vikings by the blood of the martyrs is a long one. During this process Pict and Gael became one people under one High King in their desperate bid to resist the common enemy. In addition, King Alfred of Wessex showed how a Christian monarch could use the administrative resources of the Church to help defend his people. Many monks and most priests were literate by this time. They provided King Alfred with an efficient Civil Service which administered, with honesty, taxation throughout the kingdom. This provided the financial muscle without which no army could long remain in the field. Throughout southern England defensive strongpoints were established and garrisoned. The crack troops of the Royal household may have held the centre of the Wessex shield-wall against the Vikings, but every parish sent its enthusiastic militia to beat back the invaders. Alfred was even provided with enough resources to establish a powerful navy with seamanship and courage equal to the Viking threat. And thus the southern English of Wessex held their own, but they could do little to help their Northumbrian kin to the north.

In 883 AD, when the barbarity of the Vikings was at its worst, the monks of Lindisfarne abandoned the ruins of their island monastery. They took with them the venerated relics of Bishop Cuthbert. (It was not until AD 1017 that the many wanderings of Cuthbert's coffin ceased.)

By 883, the Vikings had made England, from the Thames to the Tees, into their Danelaw where the only authority was that of the Vikings. Or was it?

The might of the Roman state had tried to destroy the infant Church of Christ and had failed. The early Anglo-Saxons who followed were no more gentle to the Church they found in Britain when Roman power collapsed, but they too could not destroy the bride of Christ. In time they too bent the knee to the High King of Heaven. During the years that Cuthbert's coffin was being carried from place to place, slowly but surely the authority of the Vikings was being eroded by a higher power, the power of God. Danelaw came to accept the new law of Christ. The terrible wars of the Viking centuries were coming to an end.

As Cuthbert's coffin was lowered into its new and final resting place, it was a symbol of a new and growing peace. Northumbrian monks began to re-build 'Hwit Herne', a new Whithorn, on a hump-back ridge of land surrounded on three sides by a loop of the River Weir. This Durham, of the much smaller Northumbria, was to continue with York of the Danelaw as the two great centres of northern English religious life into the future.

Meanwhile the Cymri of Strathclyde made Glasgow into the hub of their continuing life of worship. Whithorn was reclaimed from the Viking pirates and—like Iona and Lindisfarne—new monastic buildings were erected to stand throughout the mediaeval centuries. At this time, Dunkeld on the Tay rose to prominence in the Scottish kingdom of the united Picts and Gaels.

The Viking threat from the sea had forced religious centres that had survived their piracy unmolested to retreat inland, but with the new years of peace, it was St Andrews on the coast which eclipsed Dunkeld, Glasgow and Whithorn.

Whithorn, Iona and Lindisfarne were far from the administrative centres of the new Roman Catholic Church that grew out of the ashes of the Viking years. But these three beautiful and remote places had played their part in the Celtic Saga—the Saga of Christ—in these western isles beyond the edge of the continent. In the centuries that followed, each was to retain a strong fascination for those pilgrims who, like Columba, were searching for the place of their personal resurrection.

CONCLUSION

SINCE NINIAN and Columba's day there have been other men of great vision: Luther, Calvin and Loyola, for example, were to change the religious map of Europe in the centuries which followed. As for our century—well, ours is a secular age, the age of the internal combustion engine, electronic communication: technology has advanced beyond belief. Or has it? The world we inhabit is now a struggling and poisoned planet. War, destruction and hatred have blighted the centuries—nothing new.

But running back into the past is a golden, unbroken thread of exultancy in a Kingdom that contradicts the petty atrocities of this world's kingdoms. This thread can be traced back to beginnings that must have been lovely and awesome in the origins of Lindisfarne, Iona and Whithorn.

The message of these places was heeded by the barbarity of years long ago. Let us hope that message will endure to contradict the new barbarism of this modern age, a barbarism which taints the air, the water and the very soil of this earth.

Those men and women of the early Church shone in the darkness and have never been overwhelmed. They never fought

darkness with light, for violence is not in the nature of light. Rather they overwhelmed darkness by making that light stronger. That light, still shining like the luminous *Candida Casa* of Ninian, is the Hope of the World.

Thus it does us all good to remember the achievements of Whithorn, Iona and Lindisfarne: these places still inspire us with the courage to believe in the ultimate Victory of Christ, the High King of Heaven, who will always work to break the stranglehold of evil upon His people.

ACKNOWLEDGMENTS

The Publisher would like to acknowledge the following contributors and sources for material used in this publication:

John McWilliam—for the cover design
and the illustrations on pages 1, 3, 4, 8, 9, 10, 13, 14, 19, 21 and 28
Paul Turner—for the photographs on the inside covers, pages iv, 5, 21, 24 and 27
Marianna Lines—for the photograph on page 16

The illustrations on pages 1, 3, 9, 14 and 21 are based on details from
The Lindisfarne Gospels, late seventh century.
The illustrations on pages 13 and 28 are based on *The Book of Kells*,
late eighth century.

The quote on page 6-7 comes from
Kazantkakis, *The Last Temptation of Christ*
The quote on page 21 comes from
Arthur Bryant, *Set in a Silver Sea*, Collins: London, 1900

The Author would also like to acknowledge the work of
Greenpeace and *Friends of the Earth*
—sources of inspiration for this book—